TO MY FRIEND: Rose Holton

WITH LOVE: Sally Kennedy

DATE: 7/27/16

A FRIEND LOVES at all TIMES

HARVEST HOUSE PUBLISHERS
EUGENE, OREGON

A Friend Loves at All Times

Text copyright © 2015 by Harvest House Publishers

Published by Harvest House Publishers
Eugene, Oregon 97402
www.harvesthousepublishers.com

ISBN 978-0-7369-6404-3

Design and production by Dugan Design Group,
Bloomington, Minnesota

Printed in China.

14 15 16 17 18 19 20 21 22 23 /DS/ 10 9 8 7 6 5 4 3 2 1

Yes, we must ever be friends,
& of all
who offer you

FRIENDSHIP

Let me be ever the first,
the truest, the nearest
& dearest!

HENRY WADSWORTH LONGFELLOW

The better part of one's life
consists of his friendships.

ABRAHAM LINCOLN

Blessed are they who have the gift of
making friends, for it is one of God's best
gifts. It involves many things, but above all,
the power of going out of one's self, and
appreciating whatever is noble and loving in
another.

THOMAS HUGHES

A true friend…advises justly, assists readily,
adventures boldly, takes all patiently,
defends courageously, and continues a
friend unchangeably.

WILLIAM PENN

ONE OF THE MOST BEAUTIFUL

QUALITIES
of TRUE
FRIENDSHIP
is to
UNDERSTAND
and to be
UNDERSTOOD.

LUCIUS ANNAEUS SENECA

A FRIEND IS ONE WHO *Knows* YOU AND LOVES YOU JUST THE Same.

ELBERT HUBBARD

As gold more splendid
from the fire appears;
Thus friendship brightens
by the length of years.

THOMAS CARLYLE

Two can accomplish more than twice
as much as one, for the results can be much better.
If one falls, the other pulls him up…

ECCLESIASTES 4:9,10

Perhaps the most delightful friendships are those
in which there is much agreement,
much disputation, and yet
more personal liking.

GEORGE ELIOT

7

Oh, the comfort, the inexpressible comfort of feeling safe with a person, having neither to weigh thoughts nor measure words, but pouring them all right out, just as they are, chaff and grain together...

DINAH MARIA MULOCK

Man's best support is a very dear friend.

CICERO

But remember this, when we make the biggest fools of ourselves that is precisely the time when we need friends, and when they stick to us the tightest, if they are worthwhile.

GENE STRATTON-PORTER

But Friendship is the BREATHING ROSE, with Sweets in Every Fold.

OLIVER WENDELL HOLMES

God is **MY HELPER.**
HE IS A
FRIEND
OF **MINE.**

Psalm 54:4

Friendship only is, indeed, genuine when
two friends, without speaking a word
to each other, can nevertheless find
happiness in being together.

GEORG MORITZ EBERS

Stay is a charming word in a
friend's vocabulary.

AMOS BRONSON ALCOTT

Of all the music that reached farthest
into heaven, it is the beating of a loving
heart.

HENRY WARD BEECHER

I thank God for you!

WE HAVE BEEN
FRIENDS
TOGETHER
in sunshine
AND IN SHADE.

CAROLINE E. S. NORTON

What greater thing is there for two
human souls than to feel that they
are joined—to strengthen each
other—to be at one with each other in silent
unspeakable memories.

GEORGE ELIOT

For delays and hindrances may bar the
wished-for end;
A thousand misconceptions may prevent
Or could from coming near enough
to blend;
Let me but think we have the same intent,
That each one needs to call the other, "friend!"

AMY LOWELL

Verily great grace may go with a little gift and
precious are all things that come from friends.

THEOCRITUS

Love is all very well in its way, but friendship is much higher. Indeed, I know of nothing in the world that is either nobler or rarer than a devoted friendship.

OSCAR WILDE

The best friend is he that, when he wishes a person's good, wishes it for that person's sake.

ARISTOTLE

Could we see when and where we would meet again, we would be more tender when we bid our friends goodbye.

MARIA LOUISE RAMÉ

Sharing TIME with **YOU** IS **ALWAYS** a Joy!

A True
Friend
is a
FOREVER
FRIEND.

George MacDonald

We are shaped and
fashioned by what we love.

JOHANN WOLFGANG
VON GOETHE

There is nothing on this
earth more to be prized
than true friendship.

SAINT THOMAS
AQUINAS

Your words came just when needed.
Like a breeze,
Blowing and bringing from the
Wide salt sea
Some cooling spray, to meadow
Scorched with heat
And choked with dust and clouds
Of sifted sand…
So words of thine came over
Miles to me,
Fresh from the mighty sea, a
True friend's heart,
And brought me hope, and strength,
And swept away
The dusty webs that human
Spiders spun
Across my path. Friend—and
The word means much—
    So few there are who reach
        Like thee, a hand…

ELLA WHEELER WILCOX

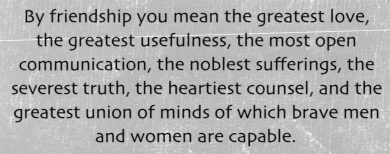

By friendship you mean the greatest love,
the greatest usefulness, the most open
communication, the noblest sufferings, the
severest truth, the heartiest counsel, and the
greatest union of minds of which brave men
and women are capable.

JEREMY TAYLOR

I consider you as a friend, who will
take me just as I am, good, or bad,
or indifferent.

JAMES BOSWELL

When a friend is in trouble, don't annoy him by
asking if there is anything you can do. Think up
something appropriate and do it.

EDWARD W. HOWE

The greatest
LOVE
is shown when
a person lays down his life
for his friends.

JOHN 15:13

THE Fragrance ALWAYS IN THE STAYS HAND THAT GIVES THE Rose.

GEORGE WILLIAM CURTIS

Friendship is the holiest of gifts.
God can bestow nothing more sacred
upon us! It enhances every joy,
mitigates every pain. Everyone can
have a friend who himself knows
how to be a friend.

CHRISTOPH AUGUST TIEDGE

Of all the best things on the
earth, I hold that a faithful friend
is the best.

OWEN MEREDITH

A true friend is the greatest of all
blessings, and that which we take the
least care of all to acquire.

FRANÇOIS DE LA ROCHEFOUCAULD

Who shall explain the
extraordinary instinct that tells us,
perhaps after a single meeting,
that this or that particular person in
some mysterious way matters to us.

ARTHUR C. BENSON

You always know just what to say

to brighten my day.

The greatest sweetener of human life is
Friendship. To raise this to the highest
pitch of enjoyment, is a secret which but
few discover.

JOSEPH ADDISON

WHAT IS A

FRIEND?

I WILL TELL YOU...

It
is Someone
WITH WHOM
YOU
Dare to
be
YOURSELF.

FRANK CRANE

I want a warm
and faithful friend

To cheer the
adverse hour,

Who ne'er to
flatter will descend

Nor bend the
knee to power—

A friend to
chide me when
I'm wrong,

My inmost
soul to see,

And that my
friendship proves
as strong

For him as
his for me.

JOHN QUINCY
ADAMS

Friends are
who ought
on a
to perservere
a

Friendship improves happiness and abates
misery, by the doubling of our joy
and the dividing of our grief.
CICERO

as companions journey, to aid each other in the road to happier life.

PYTHAGORAS

Friendship is a strong and habitual inclination in two persons to promote the good and happiness in one another.

EUSTACE BUDGELL

MY ONLY SKETCH, PROFILE, OF

Heaven

IS A LARGE, BLUE SKY,

bluer and larger than the biggest I have seen in

JUNE, AND IN IT ARE MY

FRIENDS—*all of them...*

EMILY DICKINSON

When I pray for you,
my heart
is full of joy...

PHILIPPIANS 1:4

There are souls in this world
who have the gift of finding
joy everywhere, and leaving it
behind them when they go.

FREDERICK WILLIAM FABER

No friendship is an accident.

O. HENRY

*You are always in
my heart.*

How
goodness
heightens
beauty!

HANNAH MORE

A reassuring presence,
A light when times are dark,
A hand reaching out,
Is what friendship is about.

AUTHOR UNKNOWN

I am with you.
Do not be dismayed.
I am your God.
I will strengthen you;
I will help you;
I will uphold you...

ISAIAH 41:10

A FRIEND

IS ONE

BEFORE WHOM I May THINK ALOUD.

RALPH WALDO EMERSON

The most I can do for my friend is simply
to be his friend. I have no wealth to
bestow on him. If he knows that I am
happy in loving him, he will want no
other reward. Is not friendship
divine in this?

HENRY DAVID THOREAU

Joy is not in things;
it is in us.

RICHARD WAGNER

Life is to be fortified by many friendships.
To love and to be loved is the greatest
happiness of existence.

SYDNEY SMITH

If I had a rose for every time I
thought of you, I'd be picking roses
for a lifetime.

SWEDISH PROVERB

There is no friend like an old friend who has shared
our morning days, no greeting like his welcome,
no homage like his praise.

OLIVER WENDELL HOLMES

May God's love and the Holy Spirit's
friendship be yours.

2 CORINTHIANS 13:14

Life is made up, not of great sacrifices or duties,
but of little things, in which smiles
and kindness, and small obligations
given habitually, are what win and
preserve the heart, and secure comfort.

SIR H. DAVY

HOLD A *True Friend* with both *Your Hands.*

NIGERIAN PROVERB

LIFE IS SO
SHORT
& friendship
SO PRECIOUS!

JULia
WARD HOWe

Where there is hatred, let me sow love.
Where there is injury, pardon.
Where there is doubt, faith.

SAINT FRANCIS OF ASSISI

Friendship! The precious gold of life
By age refined, yet ever new;
Tried in the crucible of time
It always rings of service true.

Friendship! The beauteous soul of life
Which gladdens youth and strengthens age;
May it our hearts and lives entwine
Together on life's fleeting page.

JOSEPH SHAYLOR

Celebrate love. It is the breath of
your existence and the best of all
reasons for living.

AUTHOR UNKNOWN

I awoke this morning with devout
thanksgiving for my friends, the old
and the new. Shall I not call God the
Beautiful, who daily showeth himself so
to me in his gifts? I chide society,
I embrace solitude, and yet I am not so
ungrateful as not to see the wise, the
lovely, and the noble-minded, as from
time to time they pass my gate. Who
hears me, who understands me, becomes
mine,—a possession for all time.

RALPH WALDO EMERSON

When hand grasps hand, eye lights eye
in good friendship
and great hearts expand, and grow one
in the sense of this world's life.

ROBERT BROWNING

FRIENDS are the SUNSHINE of LIFE.

JOHN HAY

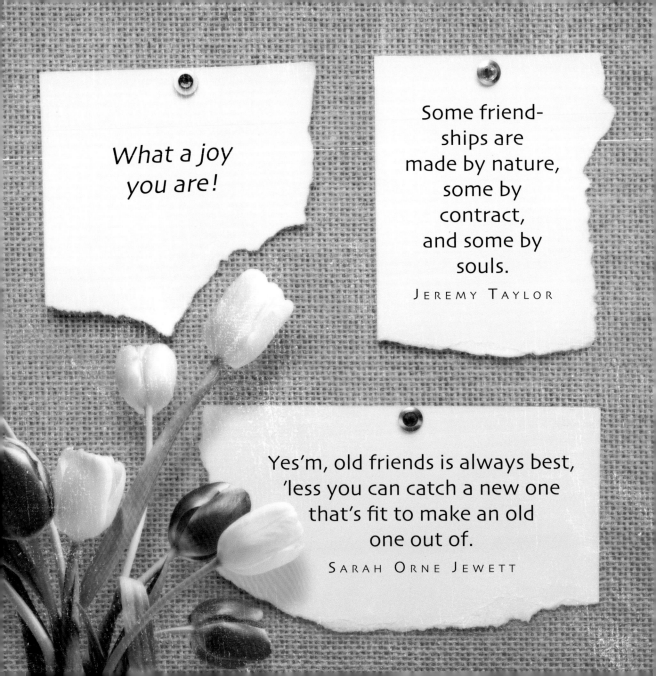

What a joy you are!

Some friend-
ships are
made by nature,
some by
contract,
and some by
souls.

JEREMY TAYLOR

Yes'm, old friends is always best,
'less you can catch a new one
that's fit to make an old
one out of.

SARAH ORNE JEWETT

WHO FINDS A

Faithful

Friend,

finds a

Treasure.

Jewish Proverb

And yet your fair discourse

hath been as sugar,

MAKING THE
HARD WAY

sweet & delectable.

William Shakespeare

So long as we love, we serve; so long as we
are loved by others, I should say that we are
almost indispensable, and no man is useless
while he has a friend.

ROBERT LOUIS STEVENSON

Charity is twice blessed—it blesses
the one who gives and the one who
receives.

AUTHOR UNKNOWN

Friendship is the source of the
greatest pleasures, and without friends
even the most agreeable pursuits
become tedious.

SAINT THOMAS
AQUINAS

Oh, be my friend, and teach me to
be thine!

RALPH WALDO EMERSON

Who is the happiest of men? He who
values the merits of others, and in their
pleasure takes joy, even as though
t'were his own.

JOHANN WOLFGANG VON GOETHE

'Tis sweet to feel by what
fine-spun threads our affections
are drawn together.

LAURENCE STERNE

WHAT A
Relief
IT IS
TO SEE YOUR
Friendly
Smile!

JACOB, GENESIS 33:10

ARE WE NOT *Like* TWO VOLUMES *of* ONE BOOK?

MARCELINE DESBORDES-VALMORE

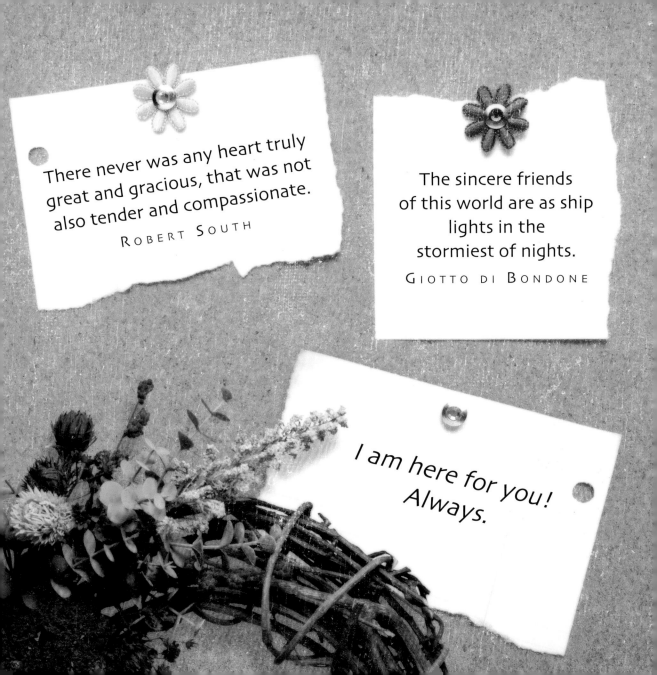

There never was any heart truly great and gracious, that was not also tender and compassionate.

ROBERT SOUTH

The sincere friends of this world are as ship lights in the stormiest of nights.

GIOTTO DI BONDONE

I am here for you! Always.

A true friend is the gift of God,
and he only who made hearts
can unite them.

ROBERT SMITH

My friend, the thought of you will be a
new motive for every right action. What
wealth it is to have such friends that we
cannot think of them without elevation.

HENRY DAVID THOREAU

When others are happy, be happy
with them. If they are sad, share
their sorrow.

ROMANS 12:15

ALL WHO WIN

JOY

MUST SHARE IT;

HAPPINESS
WAS BORN A TWIN.

LORD BYRON

A *Friend*
IS WHAT THE
HEART
NEEDS
all the time.

Henry Van Dyke